circularity

Also by Jennifer Bloom

Brainstorms
Within My Illusions
The Only Way Out Is Through
Within My Illusions (The Listening Experience)
Unconditional Openheartedness (Poetry Timeout, Volume 1)
Radical Trust (Poetry Timeout, Volume 2)
Resting in Presence (Poetry Timeout, Volume 3)
Flourishing Embrace (Poetry Timeout, Volume 4)

circularity

poems in the spirit of tarot

Jennifer Bloom

connect@jennifer-bloom.com

ISBN 979-8-9915578-4-9

Cover art: *Drink from Her Well* by Jackie Ivy, used with permission

First Printing, 2025

For my teachers.

Contents

MAJOR ARCANA 43

Foreword

Welcome to the inspired and inspirational poetry spun into *circularity* by poet Jennifer Bloom.

I am thrilled to introduce this *oeuvre d'art*—especially since these poems emerged following prompts in "The Lightning Spiral," a course I teach through Pacific Mystery School.[1] The class is structured around the Kabbalistic Tree of Life of the Western Mystery Tradition. Throughout the class we refer to the *Tarot of the Spirit*, the kabbalistic tarot deck created by mother, Joyce Eakins, M.F.T., and me.[2] The tarot is a visual symbolic representation of the One through Ten developmental pattern and step-by-step path of initiation of the Tree of Life. This sequence has been designed to move the student ever deeper into the embodiment of Cosmic Spirit, Cosmic Heart and Soul, and Cosmic Consciousness. Via these teachings, Jennifer Bloom's *circularity* blossomed.[3]

Jennifer was, and is, a brilliant, conscientious, inquisitive and mindful student and teacher of the Mysteries. It was a pleasure to work with her during the years the poetry of *circularity* was surfacing—revealing itself moment by moment both through the teachings of the Tree of Life and the experiences through which Jennifer walks daily. There is a part of Jennifer that *sees*

---

1 See www.pacificmysteryschool.com.

2 *Tarot of the Spirit* (published by U.S. Games, Inc. and Samuel Weiser/Red Wheel in 1992, along with the *Kabbalah and Tarot of the Spirit*, published by Pacific Center Library in 2012) embodies the teachings of the Western Mystery Tradition. For more information, see www.tarotofthespirit.com.

3 The structure of the Tree of Life and *Tarot of the Spirit* provides Jennifer Bloom's poetic sequence in *circularity*. The Tree of Life has 10 Spheres: Part I of *circularity*, "The Minor Arcana," has 10 parts. Part I is followed by the 4 Elemental Archetypes of the Tree of Life: Fire/Spirit, Water/Heart and Soul, Wind(Air)/Consciousness, and Earth/Embodiment. Part III, "The Major Arcana," is comprised of the 22 Paths that connect the 10 Spheres of the Tree of Life. These aspects of the Tree form the body of the Tree of Life and *Tarot of the Spirit*. The "Tarot Key" at the end of *circularity* shows the sequence with which Jennifer Bloom is working.

in poetry, a part of Jennifer that *thinks* in poetry, and a part of Jennifer whose highest *expression* is her poetry: the music of her soul. Through her writing, Jennifer Bloom learns and grows—and the miracle of all this is that, as she offers her poetry to us, we can learn and grow right along with her:

> On the first day of this journey, we travel with Jennifer Bloom, transported on a cosmic conveyor belt of primal universal light into an erotic flow of power spirals. Ignited, then, we move through layer after layer into What Is, What Has Been, and What Will Become...[4]
>
> Midway on this Journey, we discover a never-ending stream of happiness. We uncover the desire to love which creates the inspiration that comes with living in the flow of life, being in the right place at the right time, and trusting what is and what will be. The project, thus revealed, is life itself...
>
> Soon, all veils drop as we awaken the "Eye of Truth." Now, we reach the heart of absolute stillness. Now, we stop keeping score... Now, we realize that we are inside, together, and one with the Mystery—at all times.
>
> We are earnest humans, longing and loving, and realizing— yet... still... unfinished.

Though we move in circles, we are going Somewhere. In her poem "Reflection/Revision," Jennifer writes:

> Each of us is a star in life's script,
> a center of the universe in a universe
> with infinite centers, countless stars luminescing
> without daring to dim their light
> for anyone else.
>
> We are many in the one,
> constellations etched in the night sky,
> illuminating stories, the myths we live by.
> But draw new lines and reshape
> the legends of our time.

---

4 Here, I am using italics to refer to lines and concepts paraphrased from the poetic concepts in *circularity*.

I invite you to enter *circularity*. As you cross over the threshold, you will find yourself inside the house of mystery. With the first breath, you will drop into your heart. With the second breath, you will expand your awareness to every cell of your body. With the third breath, you will enter the heart of the universe—and you will know that the pulse of the cosmos is your very own rhythm.

And, now, I pass the talking stick to our master poet, Jennifer Bloom.

May Jennifer invite you in, in her own words—with her enigmatic poem "Shape Shifter:"

> I am a kaleidoscope shifter.
> Give me the pieces arranged
> and ordered and I will create
> a subtle enough force to
> shift the formation.
>
> It might look deranged at first,
> but if you wait patiently
> the components will come back together in ways
> you couldn't have imagined.
>
> I am a sense maker,
> pattern illuminator,
> dream weaver of a new story.
>
> I gently carve away masks and illusions,
> my blade softly etched
> with antique silver patina,
> more suited to slicing a wedge of brie,
> which I will also do because your nourishment
> is important to me.
>
> I invite you as my guest
> and take you under the wing of my heart.
> In that embrace you will notice
> a change.

A layer of perception clouding your vision
has lifted, and you take in more light
than you ever have before.

Join us in *circularity*, and you, yourself, will become *the living,*
embodied, essence of mystery.
This, my friend, is the change we have long since awaited.

Pamela Eakins, Ph.D.
San Francisco, California
September 2025

Preface

According to my astrological chart, my soul's evolutionary work in this lifetime is to move from reason to faith, from the mundane to the mysterious. As I turn the corner on my half-century, I can see the ways in which I've been pulled between two worlds: the material world we tend to call "real" and another world that can't be seen.

In my childhood, I loved to play in my imagination, a fantasy land where I could dream and invent realities far from the day-to-day. I led expeditions to "distant lands" my friends and I conjured in the rooms of my house. At the same time, I was captivated by the mechanics of the body. I remember learning about organ systems in fifth grade and excitedly sharing all the details with my family at the dinner table (often in song).

Throughout middle and high school, I thrived academically, especially in the sciences. In my free time, I studied astrology, read about past-life regression, and wandered through daydreams. I started college with the intention of becoming a doctor but quickly realized that I preferred talking about philosophy in coffee shops over studying in the library. Instead of graduating with a pre-med Biology degree, I earned my undergraduate degree in English Literature and later went on to get a graduate degree in Public Health with a focus on planned social change and program evaluation. I trained in social sciences research, survey design, and evidence-based methods. Meanwhile, I wrote short stories by candlelight.

In my twenties and thirties, I cultivated structure and discipline in order to navigate both a career in public health and the obligations of being a wife, mother, friend, and neighbor. My life felt meaningful. I was devoted to work that supported health equity and systems change, and I felt deeply connected in my personal relationships.

Despite all of my interests and a strong sense of purpose, depression had loomed around me for most of my life, its tendrils sometimes poking me just enough to remind me of its presence.

Other times it would take full hold, sapping life of its color and leaving me in a state of gray that even therapy and anti-depressants couldn't touch. I often felt nudges—sometimes quiet, sometimes louder—to break free from the confines of rationality and materialism.

Over the years, I acquired many different tools to support my well-being, from therapy to creative writing to bodywork. A flare up of chronic pain led me to a chiropractor who, in addition to supporting my body, recommended Michael Brown's book, *The Presence Process*. I picked it up and was introduced to a breathing practice with the mantra: "I am here now in this." I had never meditated on my own before, but I started practicing, sporadically at first, then every morning, even if it meant meditating in my car after school drop-off.

One day in 2012, I was practicing breathwork in my car when I began to sense myself both within and beyond my body. Suddenly, a flash of light spiraled up and down my spine—fleeting, dreamlike, yet unforgettable. I could *see* my spine as a crystalline container for purple-white electricity. It was far beyond anything I could rationalize.

I did what any good student would do: I researched.

Between 2012 and 2019, I took courses in neuroscience, studied Kundalini yoga, read books about quantum physics, and devoured memoirs of mystical experiences. All the while, I returned again and again to the stillness of my breath and the presence it revealed. While my meditation practices were usually unremarkable, over time I could count on them to center and uplift me. And periodically, I'd have an experience that transcended explanation.

In the spring of 2020, as the COVID pandemic unfolded, an acquaintance emailed me: Would I like her volumes of the *Zohar* (a mystical commentary on the Torah)? Since I was raised Jewish, I couldn't refuse the invitation to deepen my experience of the mystical dimension of my lineage. When she dropped the books off, she told me that she'd just started taking an online course in Tarot called *The Lightning Spiral*. The title piqued my curiosity so much that I decided to sign up too.

The correspondence course, led by Pamela Eakins and

grounded in Pamela and Joyce Eakins's *Tarot of the Spirit* deck and book, introduced us to the numerological, elemental, and archetypal patterns underlying all of creation. Each week, readings, meditations, and journaling prompts invited us into inquiry around a particular archetypal energy. Often as I reflected, my thoughts flowed into poems. What emerged was a voice that seemed as if it came from beyond my human self, a poetic manifestation of the universal mysteries through my own embodied experience.

The Lightning Spiral of the Tarot, representing the flow of divine energy through the Kabbalistic Tree of Life, served as both a map and a muse. As I moved through the cards, I began to notice uncanny synchronicities. My life seemed to mirror the themes I was studying, as if I was being offered a unique curriculum designed just for me.

This poetry collection is the artifact of that unfolding, where the archetypal journey of the Tarot meets the unique landscapes of my lived experience. I say that these poems are "in the spirit of Tarot" and not literal interpretations because, while The Lightning Spiral provided a structural framework for my exploration, I couldn't help but bring my unique twist to the process. Not every poem from those three years is included, but each one here resonates with the Tarot's numerology and archetypes that shaped my journey. Some are mystical. Some are personal. Many reside at the edge where one blurs into the other.

I believe that we each meet Spirit from our own vantage point, and Spirit meets us where we are. In this process, Tarot was the lens and I was the viewer, bringing an array of the spiritual and societal filters I've picked up along the way, including:

> my 1980's childhood,
> my suburban American life,
> my middle-aged, divorced self,
>
> my Jewish upbringing,
> my Episcopalian schooling,
> the Hinduism of my marital home,

my career in social change and public health,
my motherhood,
my creativity,

the part of me that feels astrology in my bones,
the part of me that craves scientific rigor.

Through my half century of living, I've come to realize that the movement from the mundane to the mystical isn't about leaving one behind for the sake of the other. It's more of a convergence, a recognition that both worlds exist simultaneously.

Poetry works much the same. While the words on the page come through my perspective and my lived experience, they also exist in the space between us. What you bring to the poems will transform them into something new. My invitation is to let the poetry meet you where you are and to join me in a dance between the infinitely cosmic and the intimately human.

Jennifer Bloom
Austin, TX
October 2025

Note on sequence:
The poems progress in the sequence of a Tarot deck. Each page header includes the name of the corresponding card number or archetype, serving as guideposts along the journey. At the back of the book, I've included a key for those of you who are curious about the themes of the Tarot. You can read the poems in order from start to finish or choose your own adventure. Either way, the journey will reveal the path.

circularity

MINOR ARCANA

(little mysteries)

The older gentleman sitting next to me
asked if I'm a writer.

I told him that it's one of many things I do.

"And you?" I asked.

"Oh, me?" he replied,
"I am learning about life."

All at Once

A cosmic conveyor belt of primal,
universal light transports me.
An erotic flow of power spirals
through and around me.
Ecstatic waves of frequency
pulse from root to crown.

My being is ignited.
Energy flows freely in all directions.
Universal consciousness.
Limitless possibilities.
Wholeness fragmenting into sparks
somehow
remains complete.

Simultaneous synchronicity.
Completion exists in becoming.
The end amidst the beginning.

All that is
is all at once,
s
u
s
p
e
n
d
e
d
in now
and yet forever.

Shape Shifter

I am a kaleidoscope shifter.
Give me the pieces arranged
and ordered and I will create
a subtle enough force to
shift the formation.

It might look deranged at first,
but if you wait patiently
the components will come back together in ways
you couldn't have imagined.

I am a sense maker,
pattern illuminator,
dream weaver of a new story.

I gently carve away masks and illusions,
my blade softly etched
with antique silver patina,
more suited to slicing a wedge of brie,
which I will also do because your nourishment
is important to me.

I invite you in as my guest
and take you under the wing of my heart.
In that embrace you will notice
a change.

A layer of perception clouding your vision
has lifted, and you take in more light
than you ever have before.

Missing

the ring which once adorned that finger,
I swear it was in the place
I'd left it for safekeeping
so I could decide what to do with it,
though truthfully it has lost

the feeling, the tone, the meaning
it once carried, a

link to another version of me,
far from now, removed from

the moment, distracted
by an endless scroll of
other people's lost and found,
of pop-up lists and notifications
demanding response, an urgency,
a new sense of purpose, of not missing

the mark, the boat, the cut,
which is just another way to say
something is off, not right, ill-timed,
doesn't fit, but maybe that's

the point, to feel
the space left behind by that
which is missed, the chasm
of heartache and loss, a portal
to a place that cannot be named
if I can give myself space without
filling the void left in the absence of

you.

Sacred Waters

I feel myself floating in a sea,
waters churning,
a tidal wave of iridescent foam
washing over me.

I sense a series of clicks
up and down my spine
like windows unlatching:
Click.
Click.
Click.
Click.

Click.

A rush of energy, then
wings unfurl from my back,
billowing silk
against my skin.

Now the sea is in me
and I am the sea.
I can feel it, but can't see.

I ask to be shown
some form my mind can hold onto.

You're not ready yet,
I hear in response.

You must stay in the sea and trust.

The answer is in the mystery.
The mystery is your answer.

Origin Story

We are 13.7 billion years
of creative, generative power,

the result of infinite
generations of combinations,
mergers and acquisitions,
dissolutions and re-formations.

We are electromagnetic attraction,
a falling together of particles,
of atoms, molecules, cells.

We are a compilation of everything
that has come before
and the potential of all
that will be.

Here We Are

They say that the safest place to be when a storm hits
is an interior closet on the ground floor.

When I heard his news,
sandwiched between two strangers on a plane,
reading and re-reading his message,
trying to contain my tears,
I remembered myself

back in the closet,
curled up against the wall
in the dark,
behind a veil of dresses and slacks.
A grown woman,
a mother
with two children of my own,
wishing there was a womb
that would take me back home.

But now I have unfurled myself.
I can cry across the whole house.
It is safe to look out the window
across the field of time
at all the things we've been to one another.

Friends.
Lovers.
Spouses.
Father and mother of other beings.
These words do less to define
than to mark points on a line,
the history of him and I.

I search for a word to say what he is to me now.
"Ex" doesn't quite cut it somehow,
like describing something by its absence
and ending up with what is not
and not what is.

X gives me no role to fall back on,
no rule to solve the equation:
This is what a wife does
when her husband is diagnosed with cancer.

My mind can come up with the simple answer—
I. Am. Not. His. Wife. Anymore.
But my heart doesn't understand that line.
And it's like the past twenty-five years have collapsed
into a single point in time
and there are no guidelines
when all the labels are behind us.

Except to say,
He is. And I am.
And here we are.

sorry eyes

when he says *sorry*, I feel guilty.

not for anything I've done
but for all those times he was traveling
and the thought of a plane crash
flashed through my mind,
and I felt relief.

for wishing fate would craft my escape
instead of having the courage to stand up
and open the door for myself.

when he says *sorry*, I feel guilty.

for all those times people said I handled myself
with so much grace,
when underneath stormed a rage
that I only knew how to turn inward.

for spending so much energy learning to forgive him
that I didn't even consider trying to forgive myself.

when he says *sorry*, I feel guilty.

for resenting all the tasks he's asking me to do
because I'm tired too.
and because I never learned to ask.

for wishing I was the kind of person
who could turn the other way and say,
this is not my job anymore.

for still not knowing the line between
selfishness and self-preservation.

for looking into his sorry eyes,
pleading with me to hold them
with the compassion and connection I used to offer,
and only wanting to stay there for a few seconds.

for the moment at the end of the call
when I had the urge to say, *I love you,*
but didn't.

portal

I close my eyes to contemplate
the fierce love that navigates
the paradox of hope and despair.

I see a portal open
and allow myself to be pulled
into this passage
of interdimensional transport.

"Where am I going?"
Trust.

I find joy in the movement
as light washes over me
like a gentle breeze,
streams past as I move
so fast it is almost imperceptible.
I see a black hole at the center,
just off to the right.
I feel myself shift as I round the corner
and then emerge into complete blackness.

"Where am I?"
At the center of all that is.

"Why am I here?"
To nourish yourself.

"Do I have to go back?"
Yes, to bring the light with you.

"Can I stay a little longer?"
Of course.

In that center,
I find myself held
in a peace and tranquility beyond words.

A flower emerges,
invites me to draw nectar
into my pores,
into my cells,
into my being.

Graced with the divine,
I watch filaments of light align
like iron shavings in a Magna Doodle.

"What's this?"
A *new coherency coming into form.*

Four Things to Remember

Before jumping out of an airplane
Or doing something terrifying
Or doing something exciting
Or pretty much every day

Life is a gift.
Anything is possible.
It's happening.
Savor the unfolding.

Layover

I have a thing for airport gift shops.
It's like there's this urgency to find
some item I left behind.

One day I noticed a T-shirt,
cotton soft as petals,
the washed out color of lilacs,
a white silhouette of the state where I live
and one word,

h o m e .

I thought, "How sweet."
And then, "How strange."

I cannot imagine a shirt that could fit—
my mind muses over all the variations,
as if home could be contained by
boundaries,
state lines,
nations,
or even a planet.

What if I'm just here to visit?
What if this place is just the
right nest to rest this traveler's spirit?

The Nature of Water

It might be dangerous
to let my presence linger.

I will seep into cracks

and erode the very foundation
on which you stand.

Agitated

Lately it feels like
I am being

agitated

by a
giant
cosmic
washing machine.

Particles once settled deep
within the fabric of my being
shaken free,

rinsed clean.

I only ask for a moment
to pause
between cycles
so I can brace myself
for the final
spin.

Wall of Shame

Last night I dissolved the wall of shame,
the one I had constructed to protect me
from shining too brightly.

I devised a ceremony with a balloon
I found at a party store.
It was the size and shape of a beach ball
with four quadrants of mirrored mylar
printed with the words "magical" and "shine,"
reflecting my image as a swan, a unicorn, a narwhal.

I tethered the balloon to paper tags,
Inscribed with expressions of my own internal voice of shame.
My task was to cut the cords, releasing my attachment
to those voices.

Why is this so scary?

                          Expansiveness always
                          seemed threatening,
                  but not anymore, not anymore to me.
                  I hold a key that allows me to navigate
                          through vast terrain.

What is the right way to move?

                          Guided in my knowing,
                      in the stillness and movement
                          of All That Is that exists
                  both deep within and beyond me.

What is the right way to move?

                          To follow the sparks of joy,
                          even when I can't see
                      where they are leading me.

Even when I don't know
the next step in front of me.
To follow the feeling
like hummingbirds outside my door.
Like sparrows that fly across my line of sight
the moment I open my eyes.

light

swift

free

What is the right way to move?

The way of the heart,
without expectations.

Six

Unshakeable Knowing

There is order within chaos,
　　　　　the twists
　　　　　　　and turns
　　　　　　　　　of fate
　　　　　　　bend
　　　　　　like the
　　　　　branches
　　　　　　of an oak,

　　　　　　　　　wending their way
　　　　　　　through
　　　　　　　　and
　　　　　　　　　around
　　　　　　　obstacles,

　　　　　　　growing,
　　　　　　climbing,
　　　　　dancing
　　　　across time.

　　　　　Meanwhile,
　　　　　beneath
　　　　　the
　　　　　surface,
　　　　　roots

　r　e　a　c　h　　　　　s　p　r　e　a　d

　　　c　o　n　n　e　c　t

　　　shaping,
　　　　echoing,
　　　　　mirroring

　　　the world we can see.

Snorkeling with Imaginary Sharks

there are at least two ways to enter the water.

holding onto the side of the boat,
in and out,
ebb and flow,
a call and response
like the tides.

what if there is no crisis?

                    but the suffering is real!

what if there's no conflict?

                but there are so many different ways of being!

where would it be possible to go?

                    what if there's no destination?

there was a time when I thought carefree was all there was.

the moment before jumping into the water
and the moment when I come back up for air.

the fear is still here,
but I have expanded like a sponge
with pockets of space enough for a new feeling to enter.

something like appreciation.
lightness of joy, even.
is this what it feels like to be a flying fish?

this is the part of the dream
where I don't want to wake up.
light and water interact,
muted tones give way to vibrant hues.

one solitary beam appears in the picture I take.

what is *this* light?

Whimsy

Today I wore pigtails and sang
silly songs about the weather.

Yesterday I bought eighteen giant
flowers made of rebar, painted iridescent

shades of blue and green, purple,
orange and yellow, magenta,

planted them by withering tree stumps
and called them fairy nests.

Whisper-winged moths danced
at my feet as I walked across the grass,

and I thought for a moment
that the world was a dream.

Therapy Session

One day a few years ago,
I walked into my therapist's office,
sat myself down in the brown leather chair,
grabbed a pillow from the couch
and placed it behind my back like always.
I took a deep breath,
hesitant,
apprehensive,
embarrassed,
about what I was going to reveal to her.

"I think I might be manic,"
I stated as matter-of-factly as I could.

My therapist paused before responding
in that calm, therapist sort of way:
"Tell me about your symptoms."

And so began my disclosure.

"I've been smiling all the time.
Like even when I have no good reason to smile.
Sometimes I'm just standing in the kitchen
making breakfast with a smile on my face.
That doesn't seem normal.
And I have so much energy
from the moment I wake up
until the time I go to sleep.
I'm excited to be in the day
and by all the possibilities.
I can't stop seeing possibilities
and thinking about possibilities.
It's like this incredible creative flow
is coursing through me

and I'm doing stuff with it.
Even at work, I get so excited
that I jump into conversations
with ideas and questions and
'have you thought of it this way?'
And I'm writing.
So much.
In so many different forms.
And the more I write,
the more the ideas flow.
It's like a never-ending stream."

When I finished talking, I looked at her,
ready to accept the gravity of her response.
But I found that her earlier expression of concern
had been replaced by a smile.

"I don't think you're manic," she said.
"I think you're happy."

What Is Real

The shadow of the tree is just as real
as the tree itself.

Though I might assume one to be
less or more.

They are both of the same substance,
an interplay of matter and light,

as you and I.

Now What?

I sit on a blanket looking out the window at the birds
flying through the trees. It occurs to me, as one bird comes
to perch and look inside, that I am like the animals at the zoo,
the ones inside the cages masquerading as natural habitats.

All of my comforts are tended to.
My needs are met.

I am fed.
I am watered.
I am rested.

I have playmates and tasks to keep my mind occupied,
to get me through the day with the feeling
that my life means something.

When that bird calls to me from outside,
I remember how much life is happening
out there without me.

I remember that I am not free.

But on the other side of existential angst is existential awe:

Remembering my insignificance
and the utter improbability of my existence.

Realizing the absurdity of taking myself so seriously
when I am a just a speck of matter on a tiny rock
spinning around a medium-sized ball of gas
through infinite space.

And still, I am here. I am alive.
And what is life for
if not to live it.

Unfolding

In the heart of the universe,
there is no self-consciousness,
no doubt, no fear,
no questions of right or wrong,
good or bad,
left or right,
up or down.

There just is,
and that is-ness is complete,
unfolding at the same time
in all directions.

Release the need to know.
Release the need to be right or wrong.
Release self-consciousness,
the fear of being judged
or censored
or silenced.

Trust.
Allow.
Emerge.

In the stillness and the silence
I am here.
I am listening.
I am speaking.
I am here.
Here I am.

Mission Statement

The project is life itself.

The desire is love calling me
forward in each moment.

The idea is inspiration that comes
with living in the flow of life,
being in the right place
at the right time,
knowing and trusting
the vibrations of motion and sound,
resonating in harmony
with the universal movement

toward what will be.

ELEMENTAL FAMILY

(fire, water, wind, earth)

Shape shifting,
color morphing,
there and not there,

an optical illusion
water and light
suspended in air,

refracting vibration
to reveal the unseen.

O, Father, The Expectation of Crisis

I'm startled by this field of milkweed,
which seems to have sprouted overnight
and rises several feet from the forest floor.

At first I think, *new growth; new life.*
But isn't this the same life
buried unseen for many months,
now visible in an instant?

Isn't this the new growth
of the same seed,
the original seed,
the first seed of all creation
sprouting in fractal forms
everywhere I look?

I keep reading that the world is coming to a head,
that calamity is imminent.

FIRE!   FLOOD!   DROUGHT!

TECHNOLOGICAL TAKEOVER!

THE BIFURCATION OF CIVILIZATION!

WE'VE REACHED OUR WATERSHED!

I wonder, what if this tipping point into disaster
is an imagined premonition?

What if our crisis
is expectation itself,

the idea that we're supposed to reach
one particular outcome?
But if the truth is that life has no destination,
then how can any movement be wrong?
How can any one be right?

And if we are so many captains steering
our ship toward its own demise,
perhaps we should let it be so,

let our stories fall
into the wasteland of ideas,

let our efforts and strivings
tear us so far apart
that all that's left is
an unguarded heart

so we can finally feel again
the wonder of a single moment
as sublime,

knowing that the days
will continue to unfold

with or without us.

O, Mother, Hold Us

Drink from my well, she tells me,
and I will replenish you.

Bathe in my waters,
and I will embrace you.

Let my fields caress your feet,
the dew kiss your toes
as you stroll over the undulations
of my landscape.

Let the thick blanket of my forest
shelter your spirit,
the mud that cakes
like paste on your skin
be a salve.

Feast on my beauty,
not with your eyes,
but with your heart.
Feel the joy of the sunflowers,
dancing at the highway's edge
where asphalt meets dirt.

The alignment of sun
between two half-moon rocks,
cradling a ribbon of water
cascading off a bluff, the refraction
of light off the spray.

The rust-stained cliffs, encrusted
with iron that once poured forth
from my womb, birthing life,
birthing us,

birthing now.
Imagine that.

Can you imagine that?

Can you imagine that life
is bursting forth in every moment?
Even now, when the soil is cracked and parched.
Even now, when the wounds of the past bleed open
and hearts spill out with grief.

Even now.

O, Brother, Your Majesty

I walk here nearly every day,
but today feels different.

A quality in the air.
A haunting stillness.

Quiet amplifies the sound
of birds—more than usual—

splashing around the spot where
Snowball usually stops for water,

their melodic play disrupted by a racket
beyond a thick bracket of trees.

I move toward the noise, unheeding
my mother's voice inside

reminding me that I shouldn't be
walking alone here in the first place.

Gingerly stepping on stones
that bridge the water,

I land on the other bank where
others rarely seem to go,

look around for the cause of
the disturbance and find that everything

seems in order—the stagnant stream,
the grounding tree with above-

Brother

ground roots, the pebbled
passage of the dry creek bed.

The stag's movement startles me.
I'd been looking in his direction

but hadn't noticed him in the thicket
until he announced himself

with a subtle grace that signaled
both warning and welcome.

I remember Snowball by my side
and quickly put her on a leash,

though she appears to know that
absolute presence is required.

Majestic, transcendent,
he looks at me and I at him.

And we are not afraid.

O, Sister, Listen

There are many ways to listen to the canyon.

Today the steady clicking of the cicadas
steals my attention,
soft and low at first,
modulating into a gentle crescendo,
then dropping off again.

The staccato call of a songbird,
the whoosh of a distant car,
squeals of children on the trail
punctuate the space.

But the cicadas are a constant,
ever-present base
from which everything else arises.

When my mind is still enough,
their vibration seems to emanate from me
like they are me
and I am they.

MAJOR ARCANA

(big mysteries)

i am afraid to go back
into the labyrinth.
i might find
the spirit of you

waiting,

as though you'd never left,

and my soul will beg
for me to call you out,
even knowing you and i
only exist in that mysterious unknown.

Threshold

She walked past the house of mystery,
almost too close to notice,

and yet something urged her to stop,
to turn back, to take a second glance.

Even as she wondered what treasures
lay beyond the fortress gate,

she knew that her mind
would not be able to conjure an answer

to the question asked by her heart.

Cosmic Pulse

There is nothing greater than trust
in the universal flow of life
and your connection to it.

If doubt should ever enter your heart and mind,
close your eyes and take three breaths.

With the first breath,
drop your awareness
into your heart,
and feel the pulse of love
inside your own being.

With the second breath,
expand your awareness
to every cell of your body,
attuning each cell
to the heart's pulse.

With the third breath,
expand awareness
in a 360° sphere
out to the heart of the universe,
feeling the alignment
of the cosmic pulse
with your own.

Trust your connection.
Trust your intuition.
Trust your embodied sense of timing.

Shedding

I had only planned to relax in the bath,
to let go of the day and ease myself into sleep.

As I waited for the tub to fill,
I traced a feeling back to a thought
then back to feeling again,
and realized I was ready to let go
of the me that still believed an old story.

When the water reached the right height,
I lit a candle, shut the lights,
slipped into the water, closed my eyes.

A spiral emerged in my visual field
and then another and another,
until all I could see was a web
of interconnecting spirals spinning
both individually and in unison.

A voice guided me to move toward the spirals,
so I did.

Contractions,
not from within me
but surrounding me,
moved down, around, and through me
as though I was being birthed.
The stronger the contractions
the faster the spirals spun,
becoming a vortex that would dissolve me.
Tears flowed as I felt myself letting go.
Rainbow sparks flew in all directions.

In time, as the intensity ebbed
and stillness settled in like an old friend,
I rose from the tub and put on a robe
to sit in front of the mirror.
My eyes opened into a relaxed focus.
The reflection of my likeness
flickered three times, then disappeared
like a television set that has lost reception,
leaving only the candle's glow
and a pixelated blackness.

I closed my eyes again and saw
the nucleus of an atom.

"What is that?" I asked.

The first seed of all creation, I heard.

I approached slowly,
drawn into its center,
then opened into the expansion
of all that is.

Reverence

I am the living, embodied Temple of the Mystery.

With what shall I praise this Temple?
What may I offer to the Mystery?
How might I be of service?

Invisible Work

If you're going to do something,
why not do it boldly?
If you're going to say something,
why not say it with your whole heart?

Invisible work:
The prayer.
The practice.
The offering of shelter.
The sitting together in silence.

This is my tale.
What I've lived.
What I've learned.
I want to share,
authentically expressing
the whole of what I've experienced.

It doesn't have to be for the masses.
It's not to convince anyone of anything.
Not for accolades or praise,
but to open as a conduit
of ideas, truth, love.

A punctuation mark in this story of us.

An invitation,
a place for you to settle in.
a space for pain to land,
for fear to let go its hold.

Could you allow joy
to seep into the space between
expectation and unfoldment,

for love to be what connects
through grief, through release
of disappointments,
not-enoughness,
the pressure of time
and imagined destinations?

Listen.
You might hear something
that resonates with what you know.

We are a constellation
of relational intelligences.
Nature nurturing
the technology of being,
the technology of becoming,
the face of the divine shining
through the face of you and you
and you and me.

The heart of the divine beating
through voice, hands,
pen, presence.

Until we are brave enough to meet
another where they are and say,
I hear you.
I accept your story.
Let's be in this together.

The Snail and the Butterflies

It was the snail that caught my eye,
nestled on the stem of a wilting wildflower.

I stepped closer to take a picture
and noticed the bee, which had landed
in the center of a daisy and then
took flight into the field.

I ventured into the sea of overgrown weeds,
some decaying, others full bloom.
Grass vibrated shades of celadon and jade
and tickled the backs of my legs.

The movement of butterflies,
mimosa yellow and cloud white,
stilled me enough to feel the play
of light on green as the grass
swayed in the breeze.

I relaxed my eyes to feel myself
woven into her infinite dance
of life, death, decay, renewal,
pulsing in the rhythm of now.

You and Me and We

There were three of us
in the field that day:

You and me and we,
all present and accounted for,

though at first I didn't recognize
the love standing right beside me.

I almost turned away.
I almost kept walking.

I almost forgot to say
what really mattered,

which is to say, everything
that really matters

is already here.

The Love That Makes Us Care So Much

Don't mistake my silence for indifference.
I'm trying to make sense of the senseless,
trying to figure out where my voice fits in
amidst the cries of rage, of mourning,
of intellectual reason, and demands for
#somethingdifferent.

It feels to me like we are hanging by a thread,
a fragile cord that wants to connect us
to the earth,
to each other,
to our selves.

What is the fear that frays these fibers?
Where is the love that will mend it?

Not the superficial love of a pebble
skimming along the surface of a pond,
hoping to make it to the other side without drowning,

but the love that penetrates
to ask challenging questions and listen
to answers we may not want to hear,

the love that embraces complexity,
and moves us through fear toward an intimacy
that may not feel comfortable at first.

The love that makes us care so much
that we won't keep silent anymore.

Cardiology

At first, I was there to keep my friend company
while her mom was in surgery—
quadruple bypass and a new mitral valve—
checking in daily with food
and hugs and a heart that could listen.

My timing was always perfect.
Not planned that way, but aligned
such that I was there for crucial conversations
with doctors and nurses as complications cascaded.

I watched a pulse rate on the monitor drop
from 75 to 65 to 45 to 30
as the surgeon turned off the external pacemaker,
then saw those numbers elevate again as he readjusted
a knob, setting her heartbeat back to a steady rhythm.

We joked that the electrophysiologist was so good-looking
it should keep her heart racing.
The nurse who brought us back to gravity,
detailing the procedure to install the permanent pacemaker.

Her left arm limp, she complained, "I have no strength."
It was three days before someone thought
to coordinate a visit from the neurologist,
who suspected a stroke though it couldn't be confirmed.

"Why are there sometimes two of you?"
"Maybe you had twins!"
A smile.

When I walked in on the fifth day, the room was full
of people and conversation and commotion.
I wasn't sure why I was there,

so I waited, trusting that
my presence would have something to offer.

Underneath the noise, I heard a small voice.
"Neck hurt."

I slid my left hand behind her neck.
She pointed to where her pain was.
I massaged her while holding her right hand in mine,
stroked her forehead the way I would my child's.

I wondered why it was so much easier for me to care for this mother
than it is for me to care for my own.

Someone once told me that every "Why?"
is a judgment of what is,
that hinders the possibilities of what will be.

I squeezed her hand one more time before I left,
kissed her forehead.

I cried the whole drive home and wondered,
if she is the one with the scar down her chest,
why does it feel as though my heart is the one cracked open?

Grief's Spell

As I sat brooding at the bottom of a well,
Grief embraced me like a sister
and whispered her soft spell.

There is nothing outside of now.
There is nothing beyond love.
There is nothing to fear.
There is nothing to hope for.

There is only love.
There is only peace.
There is only now.

Now is all that is.
Now is all that is.
Now is all that is.

In the beginning,
before the sun, the moon,
the heavens, the earth,
there was light.

There will be light
until the end.

Do not shun your tears, my dear,
for they return you to the ocean
whence you came.

Optical Illusion

From the subtle
to the manifest,

mystery ripples through space unnoticed,

illuminating magic in places
where just moments before
stood the ordinary world.

Date with the Beloved

Sun creeps in,
under my clothes,
under my skin,
warms the tender spots as
I lie down.

Stillness reigns.
There is nothing more,
nothing less,
nothing else
but me
in this moment.

And a voice that guides:
Lay down your knowing.
Lay down your ideas.

Until, upon awakening,
you won't distinguish
between the dream and the now.

Until, upon awakening,
you'll remember the dream
is the now; now is the dream.

Event Horizon

Out of view,
but so close I can
feel it,

a thousand-petaled lotus
unfolds luminescent,
aquamarine, pearlescent.

It starts from the heart.
It's in the heart.
It is the heart.

And though I can't imagine
a future where this all works out,
I can choose to believe in it.

A Different Answer

She says to me,
"If you want a different answer,
you're going to need to ask
different questions."

What is this world?
What is this world?
What world is this?
lingers on morning fog
and dusky evening sky.

As if the mind can grasp
an answer that is real.

As if the pathway to healing is
a puzzle to solve,
a problem to fix,
and not a wholeness to feel.

To heal is to make whole.
Healing is wholing.

Healing is wholing.
Healing is wholing.
And wholing is possible
because I am
all of me.
Because we are
all of us.
Because all is.
Healing is possible because
all is
always.

I lie down and feel the pulse of pain
coursing through me and
Why is this happening?
Why is this happening?
Why is this happening?
running through my head.

Then, a shift.
From *Why is this happening?*
to *How can I move forward?*
A new possibility.

When I let go of the urgency of my body,
I begin to sense the lightness
of dissolving into everything
and nothing at the same time.
Is this what it feels like at the end?

When I close my eyes,
the screen flickers,
and I see dancers in beige linen
twirl across a raw oak floor.
Jubilant comes as an answer
to a question I hadn't even posed,
welling tears in the chalice of my heart.

When my daughter asks,
"Do you like it when I'm at your house
or do you like it when I'm not at your house?"

I tell her that I like when she's at my house
and also when she's not.

I know it isn't the answer she's looking for.

"That's literally the most *you* response,"
she counters with an eye roll and a laugh.

I tell her that of course I prefer when she's with me,
but she asked a different question.

Would You Rather?

A small voice inquires from the backseat,
"Mommy, would you rather die in a fire or a flood?"

"Well, neither," I reply,
"I'd rather die in my sleep."

"Tonight?!?!"
my little one retorts.

"No, not tonight," I reassure her,
"I hope I'll live for many more years,
and however long it is,
I hope to find meaning in each day,
appreciate love in each being.
I hope to watch you and your brother become
the unique humans you are here to be,
and maybe even get to know your children.

Then one day, when my body is full of experience
and tired of moving around so much,
I hope I'll go to sleep and drift from Dreamland
into whatever comes next."

My young one listens in earnest,
takes in each word,
digests its meaning,
considers the idea,
and then counters,

"Yeah, but if you had to choose..."

Choreography

I am sitting outside on the deck,
legs wide, feet planted,
rooted on the warm ground.
Spine straight,
arms bent,
elbows by my waist,
forearms extended
at the level of my chest.
Palms up, receiving
and radiating.

But stillness feels too stiff this morning.
I begin to shift from side to side,
front to back,
gently rocking,
swaying with the wind.
Too much movement
and I wobble
off balance;
too little,
I freeze.

I'll play here for a little while,
learning this choreography,
dancing in the now.

Medium

Yesterday, I imagined
I was walking through a field of love.
The spring-green trees that canopied the trail,
the creek that cleansed the canyon,
the light mist that kissed my face
merely manifestations of love's grace
in this place.

Love was the spaces between the forms.

Love was the medium through which I moved
as I navigated the roots exposed
on the dark chocolate surface of the Earth,
another reminder of the web
that connects everything to everything.

Something about the way light reflected
off young leaves speckled with raindrops
called to mind that enchanted, Technicolor world,
and I became the ruby-heeled traveler
finding her way back home.

Homecoming

I am coming home to my body,
slowly,
slowly,
slowly
releasing my breath,
beginning to believe
that there is a possibility to feel
whole again.

Remembering the moments
of shuttering my self,
hiding my heart.

But here I am now
in this sanctuary I have made.
I can hardly remember those other days.

Twenty years have passed since
we shared that first dance,
that *you're just too good to be true*
feeling of hope and longing.

Seven years after I left our home,
sitting in an unfamiliar room
filled with boxes,
I noticed something
I had not felt in so long:
my breath.

And tonight, the chords of a flute
opened my heart just a little bit more,
reached down to pluck the strings
of remembering,

and through these tears I know
I am home.

66

Song of My Body

The song of my body
calls forth a promise:

I will not push through
pain,
fatigue,
weakness,
pressure,
control,
resistance.

I will tend with
love,
respect,
compassion,
care,
delicacy,
tenderness.

I will listen to whispers
before they become screams.

I will revel in each moment
of presence in my body,
right here, right now,
as perfection.

I will know myself as a fully embodied woman,
a full-bodied woman,
a finely ripened fruit, fresh from the vine
of the mystery that sourced me,
exactly in this form,
exactly in this fashion.
Each word, each note,

a new way of loving myself into wholeness,
each breath loving myself into healing,
loving myself into a new way of being.

Body image,
body shame,
body dance,
a dance of bodies
around and through
the present, past, and future.

From movement to appreciation.
from possibility to stillness.

My child self knows a secret
she dares not share,
even with her closest friends.

The miracle is now.
The miracle is this moment.
The miracle is the pulse of
yesterday and tomorrow,
here,
now,
in this single point.

Circularity

I wonder whether it's the leaves that lose their trees,
which remain stubbornly upright and still,
even as the leaves surrender
to a passing breeze,
the lessening of light,
the delicate needs of their host.

Midwives and doulas
weaving time
backwards and forwards
through ancestors and descendants,
a haunting, subtle wind inviting
the fullness of the universe
into the moment of now.

We are meant for this time.
On the threshold of relational being.

To see.
To hear.
To feel.

Sacred patience.
Presence in life.
Medicine of community.
Sacredness of all beings.

I think it is true—
the leaves do lose their trees,
wafting featherlight to the forest floor
to be returned to the soil,
composted.
Restored to whole.

Primordial Dream

A river of prayers
runs though this world,

whispered into the waters
by our ancestors'
ancestors' ancestors,

sung into the breezes by
flocks of winged wanderers,

stretching back to the time
before time

when the sacred veil was thin
and the promise of tomorrow
not given.

Sometimes I catch a wisp
of this stream, beguiling me,

floating me on that raft of hope
gifted by those who would never know
the likes of you and me,

but who were called to make their offering
to the mysterious unknown.

Praise and Grief | Call and Response

Let this be bigger than you.

> In relationship to my relationship with Life,
> this prayer seems to be opening me in ways
> I don't fully understand yet.

Let this be bigger than you.

> In relationship to climate change,
> collapse, transformation,
> however you want to name it,
> this prayer gives me space to breathe,
> to feel, to acknowledge.
>
> I am not in control.

Let this be bigger than you.

> A voice in my head cries:
> *This is urgent!*
> *Stop making excuses!*
> *You must do something!*
>
> And maybe that's true,
>
> but I read something recently
> about bearing witness,
> which made me wonder
> if that could make a difference—

to bear witness
to this morning
to setting moon,
to rising sun,
to lilting wind,
to clouds grazing sky,

to wrens nesting
on the side of my house,
to dog chewing a leaf,
to milkweed growing
through the slats of the deck,
to bottlebrush drying in the planter,

to mushrooms
blooming on the fallen tree trunk
split by lightning years ago.
Half of it grows upright,
the other half caresses the ground.

Let this be bigger than you.

When ice covered Texas in the February freeze,
a friend told me he felt sorry for the trees.
I looked out at the frozen canyon and thought,
Somehow, I think the trees will be okay.

Humans, perhaps another story.

There's a strange dissonance
in looking at what I know is there
but cannot see.

In the mountains,
a white-out landscape,
a parlor trick of Mother Nature,

to make a whole mountain range
disappear, not with fog or snow, but
a skyscape of smoke from fires to the west,

reminding me of the morning
I woke up to find my canyon
cloaked in ice,
a shimmering translucence,
where the night before
stood a dense sea of green.

There and not there at the same time.

Is this real?
Is this real?
Is this real?
How can this be real?

Let this be bigger than you.

I'm embarrassed to admit:
A part of me is filled with exhilaration,
the sheer enormity of existence,
the vulnerability and the persistence,
the beauty and the devastation.

Let this be bigger than you.

Could it be both praise
and grief to bear witness

to this moment:
celebrating the mountains
though they are veiled by smoke?

to this moment:
consecrating a concrete slab
at the edge of a cliff, remnants of a home
that no longer exists, one massive column
lifeless on the beach below?

to this moment:
dancing with the trees
and the bright, chiming melody
of icicle castanets?

Let this be bigger than you.

What comes next?
What comes next?
What comes next?

Let this be bigger than you.

When I close my eyes,
birdsong fills the whole space.
And the wind in the trees.
And gentle chimes.
A car across the road.
An engine above.

Call and response.
Call and response.
Call and response.

Living in the Future We Forecasted

One day the spring on the garage door snapped.

It was pouring, which is unimportant
to this story, except it's been so damn hot
and dry lately, and it's nice to remember
that sometimes it does rain here.

I had pulled my car into the garage
like I always do and pressed the button
to close the overhead door as I went inside.

Though now as I write this, it seems odd
to say that I went inside because
the garage is also inside, but not as
inside as the house, I suppose.
And sometimes I think it's odd
to have a whole room dedicated
to a car.
But I do.

A minute or so later
I heard a crashing sound and went back
to look in the garage, but saw nothing,
no obvious sign of damage or disrepair.
Everything was in its place.

Perhaps I had imagined the noise.

My neighbor, Wayne, knew right away.
I called him when the door wouldn't open.
"I heard a crashing sound," I told him.
"Must be the spring that broke," he replied.

I hadn't known what I was looking for.

Wayne offered to help me open the door.
But it was too heavy.
So I was stuck.

"I guess the universe wanted me to stay home,"
I laughed to myself and to Jenn over text.
I was supposed to have brought her lunch.
"It's a good day to be on the sofa with a blanket,"
she responded.

My dogs had the same idea.
Snowball sprawled on the gray couch.
Cookie conked out on the orange one.
I on the indigo chair.
Eyes heavy.

I read that most springs are designed
to open and close a garage door 10,000 times.

How many times had I gone out and in?

Reprimand

Once, someone accused me
of surrounding myself with people
who make me feel good about who I am.

And it was true.

I felt bad about it for a while
until I realized,

maybe that's the point.

Vantage Points

A bird singing on my left,
in my right mind Joni Mitchell croons,
"I really don't know clouds at all."

I open my eyes just in time
to watch a hawk fly from his perch
around the back of the house.
A moment later and I would have missed it,
never would have known
that the hawk was there and gone
or had been there in the first place.

Within me I feel a percolation
I can't yet identify.
Can I trace the outline of the form
or will I be like Joni, looking from both sides,
all sides, only to realize
there is so much more
that I don't know
than I do?

And when I emerge,
like a snake growing new skin is still the snake,
the one who is me will still be me,
expanding in scope and presence, perhaps,
but always me.

And isn't that the essence of transmutation?

Skinny Dipping

It was my grandmother who taught me
about skinny dipping, swimming in her pool
in Rancho Mirage, California, emerging
from her bedroom in a yellow terry cloth robe,
pink floral swimming cap, and plastic flip flops.

"It's my house and my pool," she'd declare
in response to my embarrassment.
"I'll do as I please."

I'd slink down the pool steps in a swimsuit
while she'd dive into the deep,
swim a lap or two before popping up
out of the water to acknowledge me
with an, "Ah, feels like velvet!"

Now, in possession of my own pool,
secluded from human view,
I float and glide, perhaps not skinny
but somewhere between fit and fat,
dipping into the warm womb of the water.

I rest my forearms on the second step,
suspend my face just above the water,
release tension.

Supported in all directions,
I surrender my weight.
The density of my body dissolves,
the urge to hold on dissipates,
the need to keep things together releases.

XII. The Hanged Man

Until rising from the water,
gravity pulls me back
into the heaviness of my form,
which only moments ago had floated
unencumbered, free.

Compost

My body rests on the cool, damp earth.
Some might say "rotting."
I prefer decomposing.
De–composing.
Being composted.
Digested,
returned to life.

What will nourish itself from my remains?
Who will celebrate the beginning
of my return to the source of creation,
each cell of my body transformed,
translated into new building blocks?

Even as my body decays,
can I revel in the possibility of the new,
the changing, the ever evolving?

The Second Hand

of the clock

is the moment

to be aware of.

The presence

of nothing

but

here now

is all that is.

All that is

is here now.

Checklist

I was just about to make my list
of things to do.

When I remembered that *I am*
is a complete sentence.

Still Time

I am trying to rush things, to reach the end before I've even started.

I am thinking about time, the agenda, my next item of business.

I am second-guessing my decision to practice now; maybe I
   should stop and come back later.

Instead, I breathe: *I am here now in this.*

One word on each inhale and exhale. I. Am. Here. Now. In. This.

My dog barks. Then quiet.
I. Am. Here. Now. In. This.

A wisp of hair breaks free of its clip, tickling my forehead.
I. Am. Here. Now. In. This.

Some creature scampers in the tree above me.
I. Am. Here. Now. In. This.

A center point emerges in my field of vision. A curtain lifts on
   the screen of my eyelids, as though my eyes were wide open.
I. Am. Here. Now. In. This.

Golden rays appear from the center point.
I. Am. Here. Now. In. This.

Filaments of light spread wide enough to engulf me.
I. Am. Here. Now. In. This.

I allow myself to be submerged.
I. Am. Here. Now. In. This.

The whole field is golden light. I am the field of golden light.
I. Am. Here. Now. In. This.

The light converges overhead, streaming in and out of my crown.
I. Am. Here. Now. In. This.

I feel the laser-focused heat of the sun beaming on my dark
   hair, almost unbearable, then relenting under the shadow of a
   passing cloud.
I. Am. Here. Now. In. This.

And there is still time.

Eye of Truth

In the small hours of the morning,
the clock's time has no meaning.

> *Slow down.*
> *Stop keeping score.*
> *Let it be what it is.*

In the dawn of a new way of being,
oneness will try to squeeze
through moments when you least expect it.

> *Drop the veils.*
> *Let yourself feel*
> *the pain, the pleasure.*

In the small hours of the morning,
the clock's time has no meaning.

> *The center of the heart*
> *is an eye that only sees truth.*

In the dawn of a new way of being,
the space of oneness will try to squeeze
through moments when you least expect it.

> *The heart of center*
> *can only be reached*
> *in absolute stillness.*

Fractured | Reunited

A wound was festering inside me,
Awakening me at 2am
To sob for an hour.

"Sob?" asked a friend.

Yes, I replied, *sobbing is essential.*
Cathartic.
Release and relief.
Without thoughts or stories.
Intimate and pure
As the night sky.

Opening my heart enough,
Clearing the space enough,
To feel the birds outside my window
Dancing inside me this morning,
To bring me back home to knowing

Fractured | Reunited
Not as binary
But as a perpetual state
Of becoming.

Feeling the universe's eternal dance of
Separation | Reunification
Within me,
From deep inside my cells
To the body that exists
Beyond my body.

Fractured Reunited Fractured
Reunited Fractured Reunited
Fractured Reunited Fractured

Reunited Fractured Reunited
Fractured Reunited Fractured
Reunited Fractured Reunited
Always forever.

Ruminating

I am walking in the rain,
rearranging myself
with each step,

with each breath,
each drop penetrates
to the depth

of the story I've dreamed,
the beginning and the end
tangled like the mycelium

around roots of weeds
that I've tried to expunge
from my yard.

What wants to be will.
And what never was
still haunts this mind's imagination.

Reflection | Revision

Each of us is a star in life's script,
a center of the universe in a universe
with infinite centers, countless stars luminescing
without daring to dim their light
for anyone else.

We are many in the one,
constellations etched in the night sky,
illuminating stories, the myths we live by.
But draw new lines and reshape
the legends of our time.

Liminality

She plays games with the ocean,
lets the surf tickle her feet,
ankles, calves, knees.
She lifts her long skirt
so its flowers are watered
only by the spray of larger waves.

The ocean beckons her.
She wades out farther only to retreat
when she feels the current pull
at the sand beneath her feet.

She watches the tides approach and recede,
cradled by black rocks and trees
that line the sides of the crescent bay
as the day's light is both reflected
and extinguished by the water.
The cloudless blue fades into a rainbow
of peaches, pinks, purples.
The moon rises behind her.

After the sun sets,
there is a sort of transformation.
When the brilliant flame
disappears below the horizon,
the sky brightens once more.
The azure hue of the day wanes
and in its place another sort of radiance surfaces,
one that holds the traces of what has passed
and an understanding of that which is yet to come.

She stands under this sky,
Watches the seawater turn black,
trees and rocks forming jagged silhouettes.

Feels her feet burrow into soft warm sand.
The cold of the ocean sends a peace through her.

The sky grows darker.
The first stars appear.
They had been there all along—
She just couldn't see them in the light of the sun.

Radiance

The feeling of exaltation comes quickly
and without effort—
crown opens, sun spirit
floods through me.

Tears form in the corners of my eyes.

I think, *There must be something wrong with what I'm doing.*
This meditation feels too easy,
too natural.

But maybe that's the message:
don't push,
don't force,
be prepared.

Let the path unfold.

Reality Check

My experience with transcendence
has brought me squarely back into my body
with a thud,

as if to say, "Yeah, well, you're here now.
What are you going to do about it?"

As It Was

What I want to say is
pain has no boundaries
and neither does love.

Nature is as ferocious
as she is gracious,
and magnificent in both regards.

This body is as supple
as it is stiff, and though they tell me,
"You're doing well for your age,"

I silently want everything to be as it once was.

As it once was before
time ravaged the horizon
and gravity wore down the soul.

I Am

the tree releasing,
the leaves amber, gold, and burgundy,

the deer crossing the path,
the human and canine looking on,

the blue jay in the underbrush,
the morning meal,

the pen gliding across
the page with shimmery blue patterns,
the ink weeping,
the story revealing,

the sound waves rebounding,
the metal chimes,
the breeze that moves them,

the flame of the candle,
the wick and the wax,
half solid, half liquid,
the release into obscurity,

the coffee grounds at the bottom of the press,
the press itself,
the water infused,
the flavor of roasted beans,

the eyeglasses resting,
the print enlarged
with no one to see,

the call of the wild,
the still of the sea,

the darkness and the vibrant,
the desert, the rain,
fractured and assembled again,
winter to spring to summer's peak,
and autumn's falling into
the completeness
of all that I am.

unfinished

time keeps passing and
I imagine myself to be
back where we started,

and wonder how we got here
from the task of

stay alive.
stay alive.
stay alive.
stay alive.

from survival
of the species,
of the tribe,
of humanity
and civilization
and planet,

when did so much complication enter the story?

I stop shopping big box stores,
but still order my planner refill on Amazon.

I go to the farmer's market,
but my food is wrapped in plastic.

I buy bananas
in Texas
in the winter.

I put the signs up in the front yard
and solar panels on the roof,
leave the back wild for the birds,
snakes, and mammals

but seal myself in this house at night,
walk on the paved sidewalks by day,
and pay my property taxes.

as if I could own the Earth.

I wake each morning somewhere
between angst and awe,
leaning into the angst,
knowing coffee will get me closer to awe.

knowing my comfort comes at a cost
to something else,
to someone else.

knowing nothing is a given
in this fragile world; each choice, each step
feels unbidden.

is that a rationalization?
of course it is.

is my life a series of compromises?
of course it is.

and still, I don't know any other way to be
other than exactly the way I am now.

earnest
human
love
failing
striving
being

unfinished

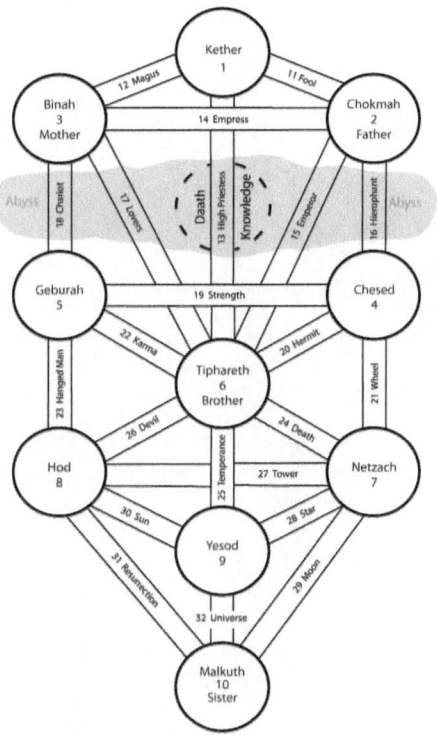

Kether
1

Binah
3
Mother

Chokmah
2
Father

12 Magus

11 Fool

14 Empress

Abyss

18 Chariot

17 Lovers

Daath
Knowledge

13 High Priestess

15 Emperor

16 Hierophant

Abyss

Geburah
5

19 Strength

Chesed
4

22 Karma

20 Hermit

Tiphareth
6
Brother

23 Hanged Man

21 Wheel

26 Devil

24 Death

Hod
8

25 Temperance

27 Tower

Netzach
7

30 Sun

28 Star

31 Resurrection

Yesod
9

29 Moon

32 Universe

Malkuth
10
Sister

KABBALISTIC TREE OF LIFE

(Tarot of the Spirit)

Tarot Key

Element	Suit	Significance
Fire	Wands	Spirit, Purpose, Action
Water	Cups	Heart, Emotion, Relationships
Air	Swords	Mind, Thought, Clarity
Earth	Pentacles	Body, Home, Materiality

Minor Arcana

Number	Theme	Poems
One	Original	All at Once Shape Shifter
Two	Union	Missing Sacred Waters
Three	Portal	Origin Story Here We Are Sorry Eyes Portal
Four	Structure	Four Things to Remember Layover
Five	Fracture	The Nature of Water Agitated Wall of Shame
Six	Integration	Unshakeable Knowing
Seven	Imagination	Snorkeling with Imaginary Sharks Whimsy
Eight	Metaphor	Therapy Session
Nine	Return	What Is Real
Ten	Eminence	Now What? Unfolding Mission Statement

Number	Theme	Poems
Father	Stewardship	O, Father, The Expectation of Crisis
Mother	Wisdom	O, Mother, Hold Us
Brother	Quest	O, Brother, Your Majesty
Sister	Curiosity	O, Sister, Listen

Major Arcana

Archetype	Theme	Poems
0. The Fool	Beginnings, openness, sacred trust	Threshold
I. The Magus	Power, manifestation	Cosmic Pulse
II. The High Priestess	Inner knowing, mystery	Shedding Reverence Invisible Work
III. The Empress	Nurturing, abundance, creation	The Snail and the Butterflies You and Me and We
IV. The Emperor	Structure, authority, stability	The Love the Makes Us Care So Much
V. The Hierophant	Soul wisdom, devotion	Cardiology Grief's Spell Optical Illusion
VI. The Lovers	Connection, union	Date with the Beloved
VII. The Chariot	Aligned will, movement	Event Horizon A Different Answer Would You Rather?
VIII. Strength	Courage, inner power, grace	Choreography

Archetype	Theme	Poems
IX. The Hermit	Solitude, insight, light within	Medium Homecoming Song of My Body
X. Wheel of Fortune	Cycles, change	Circularity Primordial Dream Praise and Grief | Call and Response
XI. Karma	Accountability, balance, divine order	Living in the Future We Forecasted Reprimand
XII. The Hanged Man	Perspective, surrendered heart, trust	Vantage Points Skinny Dipping
XIII. Death	Transformation, release, endings	The Second Hand Compost
XIV. Temperance	Harmony, balance, integration	Checklist Still Time
XV. The Devil	Shadow, illusions of separation	Eye of Truth
XVI. The Tower	Awakening, disruption, collapse	Fractured | Reunited Ruminating
XVII. The Star	Renewal, clarity, hope	Reflection | Revision
XVIII. The Moon	Deep feeling, mystery	Liminality
XIX. The Sun	Radiant joy, vitality	Radiance
XX. Resurrection	Rebirth, heart's awakening	Reality Check As It Was
XXI. The Universe	Wholeness	I Am Unfinished

Gratitude

To Pamela Eakins, my teacher, guide, and mentor through this journey. Your deep wisdom and unwavering support have been beyond measure. Bless, bless, bless!

To Joyce Eakins, whose art opens portals.

To Jennifer Hritz, my thought partner, editor, and soul sister. This book would not have come into form without you.

To Jennilie Brewster, George Gonzalez, Melanie Greenberg, and Suchi Gururaj who read drafts of this collection and provided feedback and critique. Thank you for stretching me and keeping me accountable as a writer.

To Ariel Spilsbury, Fairy Godmother extraordinaire.

To the Garrison Fellows & Mwe Council for stretching my mind to new ideas.

To Poets and Friends of Austin, Texas, for reading and critiquing many of the poems in this collection.

To Laraine Lasdon for championing my poetic presence.

To Kallie Falandays and Tell Tell Publishing for handling the logistics of bringing this book into the world.

To my Poetry Timeout readers who encourage me to keep going.

To my parents and my children for the love that we have.

To the canyon, my teacher and muse.

And to you, the one who is reading these words, for giving them life.

Notes

"Agitated," "All at Once" (as "All That Is Is All at Once"), "Four Things to Remember," and "The Snail and the Butterflies" (as "The Rhythm of Now") were originally published in *Pandemic Corona*, Sisters of the Holy Pen (Pamela Eakins, Editor). Independently published, 2020.

"Shedding," "Cardiology" (as "Why?"), and "Would You Rather?" were originally published in *Death*, Sisters of the Holy Pen (Pamela Eakins, Editor). Independently published, 2020.

"Praise and Grief | Call and Response" and "sorry eyes" were originally published in *Justice*, Sisters of the Holy Pen (Pamela Eakins, Editor). Independently published, 2020.

"unfinished" was originally published in *Liberty*, Sisters of the Holy Pen. (Pamela Eakins, Editor). Independently published, 2021.

"Origin Story" (as "Genesis") and "O, Mother, Hold Us" (as "The Radical Mother Who Holds Us All") were originally published in *Sacred Earth*, Sisters of the Holy Pen (Pamela Eakins, Editor). Independently published, 2021.

"Homecoming," "Cosmic Pulse" (as "Tuning to the Pulse of Love"), "O, Father, The Expectation of Crisis" (as "Tipping Point"), and "Now What?" and "Unfolding" (as "Emergence Part 1 & 2") were originally published in *Sanctuary*, Sisters of the Holy Pen (Pamela Eakins, Editor). Independently published, 2021.

The mantra "I am here now in this" in the poem "Still Time" is a reference to Brown, Michael. *The Presence Process: A Journey Into Present Moment Awareness*. Rev. ed., Namaste Publishing, 2010.

About the Author

Jennifer's previous publications include *Brainstorms* (poetry), *Within My Illusions* (poetry), *The Poetry Timeout Collection* (poetry, prose, and photography), *Artwise Poetry Roulette Cards* (card deck), *The Only Way Out Is Through* (songs), and *Within My Illusions* (The Listening Experience) (spoken word).

She lives in Austin, Texas, and shares poems through her Poetry Timeout Project, which invites readers to reflect on the sacredness of being alive. Explore her creative ecosystem at Jennifer-Bloom.com.

www.ingramcontent.com/pod-product-compliance
Lightning Source LLC
Chambersburg PA
CBHW021117130626
46554CB00002B/736

* 9 7 9 8 9 9 1 5 5 7 8 4 9 *